MW01717145

So Much to Drool About

Lessons for Living Large

Contents

Copyright © 2025
By Barbara Stone
ISBN: 978-1-961757-92-9

Advance Praise

Barb Stone's *So Much to Drool About: Lessons for Living Large* is a delightful and inspiring read. You can open to any page and find wisdom that encourages you to embrace the day with purpose and joy. With themes of resilience, adaptability, and independence, this book offers meaningful lessons for readers of all ages. Whether you're facing challenges or looking for a lighthearted reminder to live fully, these canine stories are the perfect source of daily motivation!

-Andréa Price

YOUR PRICELE$$ CNY REALTOR®

The 2023 Greater Syracuse Association of Realtors Shining Star Award Winner

"This isn't the first time a work has inspired me to adopt a dog, it is, however, the first time I imagined myself caring for a gentle giant of a dog, such as the beloved Danes showcased in Stone's book: *So Much to Drool About: Lessons for Living Large*. There is so much clear wisdom in this work, and with it a gentle encouragement to center oneself into what truly works in times of ease and of distress. It brings to mind the thoughtfulness of Emerson and Thoreau as well as a Mary Oliver-like capacity to see the world through a lens broader than ours. This is a work for any one of us, young or not so young, who seeks to settle oneself into a living that is rich, loving, and uncomplicated with unnecessary inner turmoil."

-Maria Sirois, Psy.D.

Author of *A Short Course in Happiness After Loss*

You had me at "So Much to Drool About." This is the title of Barb Stone's new book about the depth of what it really means to live life to the fullest. And can I say, the word that comes to mind after spending time with this book is "BEAUTIFUL." The illustrations are beautiful, the dialogue between the dogs is beautiful and the beautiful and profound mic-drop wisdom sentences go straight to the heart. Everytime.

And this is one of those books that speaks to all ages ... yes, it may appear like a children's book, yet at its core it speaks to the sage in all of us ... and reminds us who we really are as human beings on this magical path called life. I enjoyed reading and looking at every page... and will continue to as I read this and share this with everyone in my life.

-Dr. Rick Tamlyn

Hay House author of *Play Your Bigger Game*

"This book is absolutely wonderful! It teaches so many awesome lessons in the sweetest way. I can't say enough good about it!"

-Irene Scruton

Assistant Dean, School of Business, SUNY Oswego

"*So Much to Drool About: Lessons for Living Large* is everything I love about life—joy, connection, and savoring every moment. My friends perfectly capture what it means to live large and love deeply. It's a must-read, and trust me, it's drool-worthy!"

-Axel

A neighborhood Dane

Dictionary.com defines the word drool as "To show excessive pleasure or anticipation of pleasure."

Life isn't always a walk in the park—there are rainy days and rough patches too. But like a dog's unbreakable spirit, we can embrace every moment with eagerness, whether it's a new adventure, a challenging hurdle, or simply the comfort of familiar faces. Here's to living large, savoring every treat, and finding joy in the journey, rain or shine.

Foreword

There's so much to drool about in life, isn't there? For me, drooling is everything. It's not just about food—though a slice of sweet potato or a crunchy kibble might top the list. I drool over a new friend walking by, the sound of my humans coming home, the promise of a walk, or even just the sight of a sunny spot on the rug to nap in. Every moment brims with excitement and anticipation.

When I heard my friends were writing this book, I couldn't stop drooling. Literally. They've captured everything we dogs want you to know about life: how to embrace each wag-worthy moment, how to cherish your pack, and how to live large with joy and resilience.

Life is about the anticipation—the possibilities that lie ahead. And guess what? You hold all of that right here in your hands. *So Much to Drool About: Lessons for Living Large* is not just a book; it's a guide to discovering what makes life beautiful through the eyes of dogs like Jazz, Beau, Aryanna, Zeus, and me. Each of us has a unique story, and together we've learned that whether the sun is shining or it's raining (great for splashing!), there's always something to wag your tail about.

So, take a moment to savor what's in front of you, just like I savor every delicious smell wafting from the kitchen. Dive in, wag your tail, and drool over the beauty of life, because there's truly so much to live for.

Sniffs and slobbers,
Axel
One of the neighborhood Danes

Introduction

Why Great Danes?

Where did my love for animals begin? Maybe it was when I was just a toddler growing up on Long Island, where we had room in our home, our yard, and our hearts for pets of all kinds. This love has been an insatiable quest throughout my life, growing deeper with each new connection.

My first pet, Bullets, a loyal German Shepherd, was trusted to watch over us kids. We also had a duck named Poppy, but after Bullets got to him one day, only feathers remained. After Bullets came Tippy, another German Shepherd, and a series of Calico cats, all named Pudding. Our home was always open to many types of animals, including parrots, an Irish Setter named Rory, and even a Woolly monkey named Coco, who dined in a highchair and wore my mom's knitted sweaters.

At 15, my love for animals deepened when I got a horse, Wind Song. We formed a special bond, but when she became lame, I had to let her go to a retirement home. Shortly after, a Boston Terrier mix appeared near the stable, and I brought her home. I named her Windy in honor of my beloved horse. It seemed whenever I lost an animal, another would find me, as if the universe knew there was always room in my heart for one more.

The story of how I came to love Great Danes began in junior high school. I went to a new friend's house and met her family's Dane, Buckley. He was tan, massive, and loving—everything you'd want in a dog. Buckley sat on the couch with his front legs on the ground and his butt propped up like a human. I was completely taken by him, and from that day on, the dream of having my own Dane was planted in my heart.

Years went by, and after getting my own dog, Sam (half Beagle, half Bluetick), who traveled everywhere with me, I married my husband, Bob. Sam was part of the family, and soon we began rescuing other animals, including a Basset Hound named Henry and a long-haired stray cat named Pewter. Each pet had its own unique story, but they all brought the same joy and companionship into our lives. Even when Lilly, a dog hit by a car and left in a ditch, came into the picture, she fit right in. Life had its challenges—Bob passed away unexpectedly—but my furry family was my comfort during those tough times.

Life went on. My partner, Frank, and I built a life together, cultivating and continuing a passion for rescuing animals. That's how we got here. One day I saw an ad for a one-year-old Harlequin Great Dane, a trained female. My dream of owning a Dane was about to come true. I visited her, and despite agreeing to a "trial" run, I ended up bringing her home that same night. Frank and I renamed her Jazz, and she never left. Jazz was my first Harlequin Great Dane, and she lived up to every expectation. She was big, loving, and a source of endless joy.

With Jazz, our home and hearts grew even larger. We brought in more animals as time went on—like Beau, our male Dane, who we picked up as a puppy just before Thanksgiving and renamed from Zeus to Beauregard. Life with two big dogs was an adventure: bigger cars, bigger food bills, bigger vet bills, and most of all, bigger hearts.

The pattern of loss and new beginnings continued. Jazz eventually passed away, but soon after, Aryanna, another Harlequin, came into our lives. When Beau passed after living 11 years and 5 months with us, we were heartbroken. We searched for a new male Dane, deciding this time on a Blue Dane, who we named Zeus in honor of Beau's original name.

Throughout all these years, each animal has taught me something special. Jazz taught me that it's okay to take up space, both physically and emotionally. Beau showed me the importance of finding solace, even in unexpected places, like fitting his big body into my lap. Aryanna reminds me to embrace new adventures, but never forget the pack that supports me. Zeus—well, Zeus has taught me that it's okay to use your voice, even if it's the middle of the night and all you want is to be let outside.

So, why Danes? Because they are more than just dogs. They are family, teachers, and loyal companions. They fill our home with love, laughter, and lessons that remind us to embrace who we are, love fiercely, and cherish every moment. Whether it's Jazz and her confidence, Aryanna and her independence, or Beau and his gentle soul, each Dane has left paw prints on my heart that will last a lifetime. I wouldn't have it any other way.

With Love,
Barb

Lessons from the Pack

In the journey of life, our beloved companions teach us profound lessons about resilience, growth, and joy.

Together, Jazz, Beau, Aryanna, and Zeus embody the essence of resilience, wisdom, individuality, and positivity. Their stories remind us to celebrate our strengths, learn from our challenges, and cherish the bonds that warm our hearts. In their own unique ways, they show us that life's greatest lessons often come from the simplest, most heartfelt moments shared with those we love.

Not Dogs—Big Beings

"I love spending time with people," said Zeus. "Mom and Dad think that there is a difference between me and them, but I don't see it."

In the language of love, distinctions fade. To a heart full of affection, we're all just big beings sharing life's journey together.

Pushing the Limits as Creative Beings

"Every now and then, it feels like my brain gets stuck," said Jazz. "When this happens, I feel like I can't break out of going through the motions: having my dinner, napping on the floor, going out in the morning, and on and on.

"The best thing I can do for myself during these times is go for a long walk to smell new smells and even see new people! This helps me feel refreshed with new ideas and new energy."

In the exploration of new scents and sights, creativity finds its wings and soars.

Learning How to Be the Voice of Motivation

“When Jazz isn’t feeling well, I stay near her and try to understand what she needs,” said Beau.

“That’s really thoughtful of you. How do you handle it?” asked Aryanna.

“I let Mom and Dad know if she needs help,” Beau answered. “It’s tough, but I try to keep a cheerful attitude for her. I’ve learned that staying upbeat can make hard times a bit easier.”

With love as your guide, even the darkest times can be illuminated.

Letting Go of Perfection

"There was this time when I really needed to go out, but I couldn't make Mom and Dad understand, and I ended up making a mess inside," said Beau.

"Really? What happened after that?" asked Zeus.

"I was pretty upset with myself, but I learned that day that it's okay to make mistakes," said Beau. "Mom and Dad forgave me quickly, and I had to learn to forgive myself too."

"So, it's okay to mess up?"

"Absolutely. Mistakes are part of learning," Beau explained. "It's important to let go of the need to be perfect all the time. Embrace your mistakes, learn from them, and you'll grow stronger and better at communicating."

I can embrace imperfection as part of growth. In forgiveness, both from others and oneself, lies the freedom to learn and communicate better.

Accepting That You're a Work in Progress

"I see you trying so hard to keep up with Jazz. It's great to see that determination," Beau remarked.

"Thanks, Beau," said Zeus. "It feels like I'll never catch up to her."

"You know, it's not about being the fastest," said Beau. "It's about getting better each day. Your progress is what really counts."

Welcome the journey of improvement. Progress is not about being perfect but about striving to be better every step of the way.

Giving Yourself Full Permission to Be a Dog

"Dogs make mistakes every now and then, just like everyone and everything!" said Aryanna. "Being a dog means accepting the full range of emotions that might come my way each and every day, both positive and negative.

"It's okay for me to be different than my siblings or other dogs I meet. I know who I am, and I'm able to embrace every part of myself."

Own your bark and your bite. Being a dog means accepting your imperfections and wagging your tail through life's ups and downs.

Giving Yourself Full Permission to Learn and Grow

"I can't know everything, but it's okay for me to trust my instincts and be wrong," said Jazz.

"I know I can learn from my mistakes and try again.

"Growing is like a long walk: there are steep parts, pretty parts, tiring parts, and exciting parts."

Grant yourself the freedom to learn and evolve. Embrace the journey of growth with trust in your instincts, resilience in your mistakes, and appreciation for the diverse terrain of progress.

Intuitive Ways to Learn from Those Around You

"I've figured out something interesting lately," said Zeus.

"What's that, Zeus?" asked Jazz.

"I used to always stick close to Mom and Dad, but I've noticed Aryanna enjoys her alone time," Zeus explained. "At first, I didn't understand it. But then I tried spending some time on my own, too, and it's actually pretty nice. I can always go back to Mom and Dad when I'm ready."

"So, you've learned to enjoy both being with them and having your own space?"

"Exactly. It's all about finding a balance and understanding what we each need."

Learning from loved ones means understanding and embracing one another's rhythms.

Life’s Three Mindsets: From Passive to Proactive

“When I was younger and it started to rain on one of my walks, I used to think ‘I’m so unlucky,’ and mope the rest of the day inside,” said Aryanna.

“When I got a bit older, I would think, ‘Well, maybe today is a good day to spend napping after all and feel content and dry inside.’

“It wasn’t until I got even older that I realized the fun of learning to play in the rain.”

From raindrops to rainbows, shifting mindsets unveil the joy of dancing in life’s downpour.

Jazz

Jazz's journey begins in a small crate, confined and isolated for the first year of her life. Emerging from these constraints, she transforms into an expressive and adventurous soul, who is capable of overcoming circumstances and living in a productive mindset.

Her freedom is a source of immense joy as she learns to cherish every moment, from the simple pleasure of lounging in her favorite chair to the warmth of her family's love. Jazz's story is one of resilience, showing how past limitations can be overcome to embrace a life full of discovery and happiness.

Whether navigating new paths or reveling in the company of loved ones, Jazz teaches us to appreciate the simple joys and the beauty of each day's new adventures.

From Surviving to Thriving: What It Takes

"I spent most of my time as a puppy in a crate. I didn't understand why my first family wanted to keep me locked away. It was very lonely.

"During that time, I had to try to stay positive. I would imagine a future where I could run around and meet lots of new people. They would pet me and love me, and I would be free to stretch my legs.

"My dream came true when Mom and Dad brought me home."

Hope carries us from surviving to thriving. In the darkness of isolation, dreams pave the path to a brighter tomorrow.

Grasping the Nettle

"Even though my new home was different and a bit scary at first, it felt so good to stretch out and be free from my crate. I could explore new places and meet other dogs, which was exciting but also a little intimidating.

"I learned to embrace the new experiences, even when they made me nervous. Each day brought something unexpected, but with Mom and Dad by my side, I felt brave enough to face anything."

From the confinement of uncertainty to the freedom of belonging. In the face of adversity, persistence blooms into the sweet victory of finding a home.

Overcoming the Limitations of a Victim Mindset

"Once, when I was hiking with my parents, there was a huge, steep hill that looked impossible to go over.

"I tried to lie down and dig my paws into the ground so they wouldn't make me try it. It was going to be too hard!

"Eventually, I put one paw in front of the other, slowly but surely climbing until I felt like my legs were going to collapse underneath me. There were the most beautiful smells at the top and the view was amazing."

With determination, even the steepest hills reveal the sweetest scents of victory.

Learning to Be Okay with Being Unsure: Dealing with Uncertainty

"The dogs I meet at the park have such different lives from my own, and I occasionally fall into the trap of comparing myself to them.

"I'm not always sure where my path will lead me, but there's an inherent beauty in not knowing. I'm constantly open to the new experiences life has in store for me, even if they don't match the other dogs I know."

Embrace the mystery of your journey. In the uncertainty lies the adventure of self-discovery, unbound by comparison.

Are You Living Through a Life-Quake?

"When I start to feel anxious, it's easy for me to fall into the old habit of chewing on the side of the couch or drooling all over the floor.

"When I notice myself doing these things, I try to focus my energy elsewhere, like playing with my brother, cuddling with Mom and Dad, or running around outside.

"Life may not go the way I hope all the time, but I can choose to be grateful for what is right in front of me rather than letting the anxiety consume me."

Amid life's quakes, redirect your energy to play, love, and gratitude.

Embracing the Discomforts of Life

"I am enough exactly how I am."

It's all right if I'm different. I can love myself, spots and all.

How to Show Up for More While Remembering That You Are Enough

When I feel like I'm not enough, I can't keep up with my brother as well. I want to play with him, but I don't have as much energy.

"When I'm feeling this way, I try to keep in mind that my brother loves and accepts me exactly how I am, and I should give myself the same grace. I can show my brother I love him in so many ways besides just playing."

"Acknowledge your worthiness, even in moments of vulnerability. Your presence speaks volumes of love, beyond the bounds of energy and play."

Coping When Things Don't Go as Planned

"Every so often, I'll meet another dog or person that I don't get along with, or my family can't go on a walk because it's raining outside. It reminds me of the lonely days in my crate, waiting for something better.

"These moments can be disappointing, but I've learned to find joy in the little things. When plans change, I love to play with my favorite toys or watch the birds and squirrels outside the window. It helps me stay positive and remember that there's always something to be happy about, no matter the weather."

Adaptability is the leash of contentment—finding joy despite the unexpected detours.

Being in the Present

"If I find myself feeling disappointed or angry over something that happened yesterday, I chew on my bone or ask Mom and Dad to let me outside so I can run around. Doing things I enjoy helps me stay grounded and come back to the present."

In the rhythm of now, find peace in simple joys. Grounding yourself in the present dissolves the echoes of yesterday's woes.

Overcoming Adversity: Moving Beyond Circumstances

"After the dog next door passed away, I felt so lost without him. I missed saying hello to him when my parents let me out in the morning.

"Eventually, I was able to grow through the pain and show my parents how I wanted to be loved and how I could love them through life's tough moments."

Through loss, we discover the strength to rewrite our stories with love and resilience.

Finding Your Compass in Life

"My parents took me on vacation once, and while we were in the car, the road grew dark and foggy. There were so many new smells around me; I wasn't sure where we were going, and I felt uneasy.

"I knew I could trust my parents, so I relaxed. Eventually, I could smell the lake and the trees, and I knew we were going to be okay."

Amidst life's fog, trust your senses. With love as your compass, even the darkest paths lead to familiar shores.

Walk Where You Want to Go

"I might not know every twist and turn we'll take on each walk, but my nose knows the way! Let's take our time, sniff around, and enjoy all the sights and smells together."

Follow your nose, step by step. The journey brings both direction and delight.

Life's Bus Stops:
People's Roles in Your Life

"I've learned that life is a lot like a ride on a bus. I meet people and dogs who are along for the ride for a long time. Other times, they are only there for a short while."

Life's journey is like a bus ride. Companions may join for varying lengths, but each adds a unique flavor to the adventure.

Taking a Risk:
Are You Waiting for a Unicorn?

"When I was younger, I used to be scared to play with the bigger, older dogs. I thought they would be mean and aggressive.

"One day, I went over and started playing with them. I was nervous, but we had a great time together. It turns out, I can be friends with all kinds of dogs."

Dive into the unknown. The most unexpected experiences are waiting beyond our fears.

What to Do When You Feel Lost in Life

"There have been several times when I've had to navigate change in life: changes in my routine, meeting new dogs and people, and even moving to new places.

"These changes can make me feel lost and anxious.

"During these times, reconnecting with my family helps me feel grounded and secure. When I need to calm my mind, I love to sit in my favorite chair and watch the world go by. Sitting there reassures me and gives me the strength to face new challenges."

In the whirlwind of change, seek comfort in the things, people, and places that bring you solace. Find your bearings amidst life's shifting landscape.

Beau

Beau's journey is marked by a series of trials that shaped him into the steadfast guardian of his family. Born with health issues and facing early behavioral challenges, Beau evolved into a wise protector.

His story highlights his deep emotional bonds with his family and his unwavering protective instincts, which provide stability and safety to his pack. Beau's quiet strength and wisdom come from overcoming numerous obstacles, making him a reliable and comforting presence.

Through his disciplined habits, balanced leadership, and authentic vulnerability, Beau teaches the value of resilience, self-worth, and the beauty of continual growth. His journey from struggle to strength underscores the importance of embracing possibilities with hope and wisdom, ensuring that his family always feels safe and cherished.

We All Need a Lap to Sit In

"As a puppy, I was picked up from a farm far away and had a long ride in the car to get home. The journey was scary and new, but I found comfort in sitting on Mom's lap the whole way. Her lap became my safe space, where I felt secure and loved as I grew up."

Find your sanctuary in the warmth of a welcoming lap. It's the anchor for adventures, the refuge for reassurance, and the haven for your heart.

Taking Up Space

"I used to wish I was smaller, so I wouldn't scare the little dogs at the park," said Beau.

"But your big heart is what really matters! And everyone at the park loves how gentle you are," said Jazz.

Embrace your size with confidence. Whether big or small, it's about how you fill the space with love, joy, and gentle strength.

The Anomaly of Leadership

"Sometimes I'm a leader when I raise my voice. Other times, I lead by moving quietly and purposefully."

Leadership defies convention, embracing both the roar and the whisper.

Change vs. Transformation

"Change has come into my life through new walking paths and meeting new friends.

"For me, transformation has looked like learning how to be more obedient to my parents through training."

Change paints the scenery; transformation reshapes the soul.

How to Make This Year Your Year

"Whenever I feel like it's time to start fresh, I like to go for walks with my family and think about where my life has taken me so far.

"There have been some beautiful views and also snowy days. I think about how I can manage difficult times and truly appreciate the good times.

"This thoughtful time helps me realize where I want to go next."

Step into the future with reflection as your compass.

Are You Just a Gallon of Paint?

“I, my sister, Mom, and Dad are all a combination of our individual and shared experiences, which makes us unique and compatible.

“The smells that surround me on a spring day, the sounds I hear as I drift off late at night, and the dogs and people I play with are all shaping me into the dog I want to become.”

Our experiences intertwine to craft the unique and harmonious characteristics of who we are.

Asking for Help: You Don't Have to Do It Alone

"There was a big stick in the yard that I really wanted to play with, but it was too big for me.

"My sister came and grabbed the other end, and we were able to carry and play with it together."

Reaching out for help can turn the impossible into a shared adventure.

Self Leadership:
Aligning with Your Inner Purpose

"Mom and Dad used to yell at me when I got too excited and jumped on guests when they visited. I saw how frustrated it made them. I decided I wanted to be a comfort in their lives as much as possible, rather than a source of annoyance. So, I practice self-control and greet guests calmly, knowing that Mom and Dad appreciate my good behavior."

Empowerment lies in self-discipline. By aligning our actions with our inner purpose, we become agents of comfort and harmony in the lives of those we love.

Waiting for Mom and Dad to Come Home

"Doesn't it feel like forever when Mom and Dad leave?" asked Beau.

"It really does," Zeus replied. "Time seems to stretch on and on without them here."

"I never know exactly how long they've been gone, but the best part is when we finally hear their car in the driveway."

"Yes!" agreed Zeus. "That sound always makes me so happy. There's nothing better than having the whole family back together."

In the silent moments of absence, anticipation becomes the melody of reunion. The heart leaps with joy at the familiar sound of homecoming.

Connecting the Dots Between Self-Love and Vulnerability

"As I've gotten older, I've gotten sick more and more often. I know that someday, I'll go away the same way a few of my friends at daycare have.

"I don't let this stop me from living the life I have now, though. If I need something, I tell Mom and Dad. If I don't feel well enough to play with my sister, I let her know. By being vulnerable, I can lovingly advocate for myself and set expectations with my family."

Vulnerability is not a sign of weakness, but a powerful act of self-love. We can connect the dots between acknowledging our vulnerabilities and advocating for ourselves, fostering deeper connections, and setting healthy expectations within our lives.

How to Increase Energy Levels: Essential Tips

"Every now and then, I feel worried about my sister or Mom or Dad. Other times, I get caught up in the routine of going outside, being at daycare, having dinner, going to bed, and doing the same thing over again. Times like these are when I feel the most exhausted and unmotivated.

"I have to remember to drink the water in my bowl, take time to be in nature, play with my sister, and get plenty of rest when this happens. After a few days of mindful recharging, I start feeling like myself again."

Recharge, refresh, repeat. Harness the power of self-care to reignite your spark and restore vitality to your days.

Eating Snow

"There's nothing like catching snowflakes on your tongue on a frosty morning or finding the perfect stick to carry around. Just make sure to skip the yellow snow—it's not the lemon-flavored kind!"

Savor life's sweetness one snowflake at a time.

Remembering to Dream

"It's nice playing with my sister and walking with my family, but every now and then, I don't feel well. When I'm sick, I think about all of the things I'll want to do when I'm healthy again."

Even in the shadows of sickness, let dreams light the path to brighter days ahead.

Are We Daydreaming Enough?

"I love lying in a sunny part of the house and thinking about chasing squirrels, going for a hike, and sitting on my mom's lap."

Let imagination roam in the warmth of the sun. Daydreams paint the canvas of possibility with hues of adventure and comfort.

Checking In to Avoid Checking Out

"Today I need a day to do nothing but nap. These kinds of days help me recharge, take quiet time for myself, and think about all the wonderful people in my world.

"After I have this day, I will be more ready to spend time with my friends and family and play full force!"

Taking a break isn't giving up. It's recharging to play harder.

Why Healing Is Not a Linear Process

“Playing with my new friends is great, but some days I miss my old friends who are gone now.

“I know that someday, it won’t hurt as much when I remember them and that there will be times that are harder than others. For now, I try to think fondly of the times we shared and seek out love from my family when I need it.”

Healing is a journey of peaks and valleys. In the ebb and flow of memories, you can find comfort in love’s enduring embrace.

Aryanna

Aryanna's journey is one of fierce independence and playful rebellion. As a puppy, she was stubborn and less affectionate, always eager to assert her dominance and explore the world on her own terms. Her joy in simple pleasures and adventurous spirit often led her to take on challenges.

Aryanna's transformation into a more loving and attentive dog as she grew older highlights her personal growth and self-discovery. She learned to balance her free-spirited nature with her responsibilities and relationships at home, accepting her individuality while finding unique ways to express love.

Through her journey, Aryanna teaches the importance of self-acceptance and staying true to oneself. By embracing her true nature and evolving through life's experiences, she finds profound personal fulfillment and joy.

Motivation vs. Momentum

"Mom and Dad had me work with a trainer for a while, and I didn't want to do what they asked me to. I didn't always understand what they wanted.

"They worked with me for so long, we got to know each other, and I learned what they needed from me. I loved connecting with them and listening better to Mom and Dad too."

From resistance to resonance, the dance of understanding transforms motivation into the unstoppable momentum of partnership.

Harnessing the Power of Fear

"I feel fear when I hear something in the yard but can't tell what it is. It's scary to me to smell something and not recognize whether it's a threat to my house and family.

"After years of practice, I know now that fear is how I keep myself and my family safe. Once I investigate a sound or smell further, I know I've done my job of protecting those who are most important to me."

Fear, a guardian's instinct, guides vigilance in the night.

Going to the Vet

"My mom has to take me and my siblings to the vet every so often, and I wish I didn't have to go.

"Even though it's scary, and I don't know what's going to happen, I know my mom would never put me in harm's way. She tells me that I can trust the doctor to help me, and that everyone is there to keep me safe."

Even when things are scary and uncertain, trust that those who care for you have your best interests at heart.

Understanding and Expanding Your Comfort Zone

"I feel relaxed when I'm with my siblings and parents, when I'm at my house, and in my yard. But I wonder what's happening down the street or over the fence.

"It's a little scary, but I love adventuring outside of my house and finding new smells."

Comfort thrives within familiarity, but true growth blossoms beyond its borders. Dare to explore the unknown and expand the horizons of your comfort zone.

Trusting Your Gut—Not Your Anxiety

"Late one night, I heard something outside. There was a figure moving like a shadow in the dark.

"I was so scared, I wanted to run away. But I know it's my job to protect my family, so I barked loudly, and they ran.

"I knew something wasn't right, and I'm glad I made my voice heard."

Amidst fear's whispers, trust in the roar of your instincts. Sometimes the loudest bark protects the ones you love.

Effectively Tackling Your Self-Centered Tendencies

"Aryanna, remember when you used to hide your toys and keep to yourself?" asked Zeus.

"Yeah, I was scared you all wouldn't want me around," said Aryanna. "Now I know you're my family. All of you are always there for me."

"It's great to see you so happy and part of the pack!"

Transforming fear into family. In the embrace of love, selfish tendencies yield to the joy of sharing and belonging.

Embracing New Beginnings

"It's okay to be nervous in a new situation.

"At times, you have to trust others you may not know."

Embrace the discomfort of new beginnings. Trust in the process and lean on others to navigate the path from anxiety to achievement.

Learning to Go with the Flow

"I was very stubborn as a puppy, and when my big brother Beau couldn't come to daycare with me anymore, I didn't want to go.

"I eventually trusted that Mom and Dad wanted what was best for me and learned to trust them more. I can adapt to new circumstances, scents, and places."

Flowing with life's changes, trust becomes the current guiding us through unfamiliar waters.

Finding Balance: Guarding and Enjoying Life

"I protect my house and my family and bark at things outside that I don't recognize.

"Being on high alert so much of the time is tough work, so to relax, I chew on my bone, roll around in the grass, and take naps."

Explore the balance between responsibilities and taking time to savor life's simple pleasures.

Watering Yourself Down for Others: The Importance of Authenticity

“I don’t really blend in with the crowd. Some dogs and people may be intimidated by me at first because of my strong will.

“I don’t let this stop me from being myself, though. My thoughts and personality are parts of me, and I can play with dogs and people of any kind!”

Authenticity shines brightest when you embrace every aspect of yourself unapologetically.

Visualization: Believe It to See It

"I have vivid dreams. Sometimes I bark while I'm dreaming and wake myself up!

"I dream about chasing cats and rabbits and playing with my siblings."

Dream big, bark loud. In the realm of imagination, every chase and play are within reach.

Normal Is Overrated

"Some might find it strange that I enjoy drinking from my parents' coffee cups. Apparently, most dogs don't drink coffee.

"I don't mind enjoying things that other people don't understand. It's a part of who I am!"

Get to know your unique brew. In a world of norms, be the delightful quirks that add flavor to life.

Self Check-in:
Comparing Yourself to Others

"I have friends who are very social and know lots of other dogs and people. I like other dogs, but I also like spending time by myself and with Mom and Dad.

"Some days I wish I was as friendly as those other dogs. However, I try to remember that I love being soft and gentle because it is who I am. It's okay for me to love being myself."

Between the cacophony of comparisons, find solace in the harmony of self-acceptance. Embracing your unique melody makes the symphony of life richer.

Playing with the Big Dogs

"I love to go out and find my own experiences, big and small. I always remember, though, that my family is there, cheering me on."

Accept the thrill of new adventures but keep the pack in sight. With their support, even the biggest dogs can soar.

Mastering the Art of 'Yes, And...'

"At some point during the day, my parents will ask me to sit. I don't always feel like sitting, but occasionally I like to sit and then give them my paw, so they know I'm listening to them."

'Yes, And...' is like offering a paw: a gesture of understanding and connection.

Recognizing and Appreciating the Gift of Free Time

"Some days are so busy—my family and I are running around, going to different places, or we're at home hosting different people.

"Other days, I get to relax. I can play with my brother, chew on my bone, and take a nap.

"Both types of days have become so precious to me. One fills my heart with joy and purpose, the other allows me to reflect, recharge, and reconnect with myself."

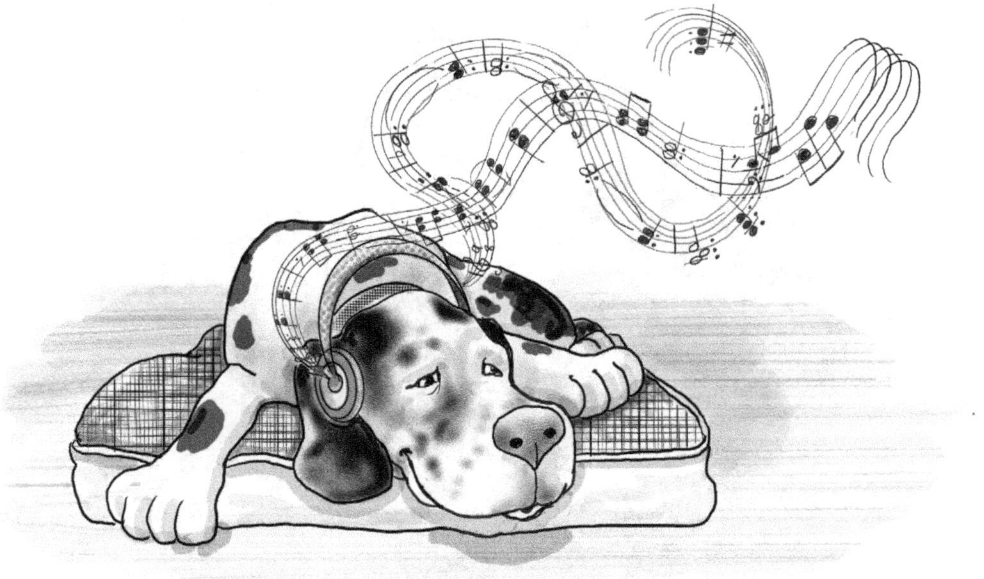

Balancing hustle and harmony: amidst the whirlwind of activity and the calm of solitude, every moment becomes a cherished opportunity for growth and contentment.

Living Life to the Fullest: Finding Your Best Self

"I love being independent. Mom and Dad were surprised at first, but they accepted it. I found my own ways, and they love me for who I am. Not all dogs understand me, but that's okay. I make friends with those that do."

Accept your unique self and find your tribe. In acceptance lies the truest expression of love and friendship.

Dinnertime

"Dinnertime is my favorite. It's so nice to be close to everyone," said Zeus.

"Yes, it's the best part of the day," Aryanna agreed. "Sitting here, we get to feel the love and warmth of our family, and it makes our pack feel complete."

In the cozy warmth under the dinner table, our family feels whole, and our hearts are at peace.

Why Loving Yourself Is Vital for Success—and How to Start

“Zeus, you know how much Mom and Dad love us with their treats and pets?” asked Aryanna.

”Yeah, it’s the best!” exclaimed Zeus.

“I’ve learned that loving myself is just as important. I take breaks when I need them and find ways to relax.”

As you embrace your worth, the world echoes back the love you’ve nurtured within.

Zeus

Zeus, the bright young mind of the family, embodies the essence of a playful and affectionate younger brother. He seamlessly integrates into his environment, showcasing remarkable adaptability and positivity.

Zeus's journey is marked by his acceptance of making mistakes and learning from them, fostering a growth mindset that inspires others. As he navigates choices and gains confidence in voicing his needs, Zeus's enthusiasm for new experiences shines through. His journey highlights the importance of family support, collaboration, and embracing one's natural talents.

With a positive influence on others and a deep understanding of contentment and cooperation, Zeus encourages us to find joy in everyday activities and to always look forward to the endless possibilities that lie ahead.

Using Butts for Pillows

"My favorite pillow is my sister's butt. She likes to spend a lot of her time alone, but resting my head on her provides a moment of connection and comfort that we both appreciate."

Finding solace in unexpected places: even a tail end can offer the warmth of companionship and the softness of belonging.

Understanding Relationships: The Parts of Ourselves

"I love how fast I can run and how I fit perfectly in Mom's and Dad's laps. I love my soft fur and long tail.

"Knowing what I love about myself helps me realize what I love about others too."

Embrace the beauty of self-discovery. By loving ourselves, we learn to appreciate the unique qualities in others.

A Beginner's Guide to Trying Something New

"Today, my mom took me in the car to somewhere I had never been before. The smells were all so new, but then I found someone to play with. If I got nervous, Mom was always there to pet me and tell me everything was okay.

"I can't wait to try something new tomorrow!"

Dive into the adventure of new experiences. Each step forward is filled with the comfort of support and the joy of discovery.

Learning and Growing: Living Life as an Experiment

"Living life immersed in the smells, tastes, and sights all around me makes me feel happy and grounded. Each new day brings an opportunity for an experience I've never had before, whether it be meeting a new friend, trying a new treat, or learning something I didn't know before."

Seize every opportunity to discover the joy of new experiences and the wisdom they bring.

Researching Yourself: The Incredible Necessity of Constant Discovery

"My parents let me outside when it was raining once. It was a little cold and wet, but I loved splashing in the puddles and squishing through the mud. That day, I learned that I love playing in the rain!"

Accept the joy of self-discovery. Like playing in the rain, each moment of exploration reveals a new facet of who you are.

Living in the Land of Possibilities

"Whether it's leaping fearlessly into the unknown or simply greeting each day with an open heart, I embody the spirit of possibility.

"Every stranger I meet is a potential friend, every new scent a clue to unravel, and every unexpected twist of fate a chance to rewrite the story of my own existence."

Explore the endless horizons of possibility. In each moment lies the potential for new connections, discoveries, and adventures.

Choices

"If I have to pick between my dog food, the butter that's on the counter, or the meat that Dad is eating, how do I choose?

"I want them all, but I can only pick one."

Amidst tempting choices, choose wisely. The path to satisfaction lies in the decision that nourishes both body and soul.

Learning How to Follow Your Life's Path

"My parents were carrying things into the kitchen, and they dropped a few pieces of food along the way."

Life leaves breadcrumbs. Follow them and see where they lead.

How to Lead with an Abundance Mindset

"My sister and I fight over our toys, especially if she has the bone that I want.

"We get along much better when I realize that we have so many toys in our house, and we can both play with different things."

Leading with abundance transforms sibling rivalry into shared joy.

Are You Doing What Makes You Feel Free?

"Aryanna, do you ever get that rush of energy when you run?" asked Zeus.

"Oh, absolutely!" said Aryanna "It's like the world fades away and all that matters is the wind and the ground beneath my paws."

"There's something so invigorating about it, right? It feels like every bit of stress just melts away."

"Exactly! In those moments, I'm truly alive. It's my way of recharging, of feeling like myself again."

"I know what you mean," agreed Zeus. "Running helps me shake off the heaviness of a long day. It's my way of finding joy and contentment again."

Feel the liberation of your spirit. In the rush of wind and the boundless expanse, find the freedom to rediscover joy.

What Is an Abundance Mindset?

"My morning routine is my favorite part of the day—there are endless possibilities for what might happen!

"Today I could go for a walk, go to doggie daycare, take a nap with my sister, get pets from Mom and Dad, enjoy a treat, and so many other amazing things!"

Discover the potential of each new day. With an abundance mindset, every moment is a treasure trove of possibilities waiting to be uncovered.

Breaking Down the Planning Process

"A few years ago, I buried my favorite bone in the backyard. One day, I wanted to have a friend to share my toys with.

"I kept visualizing the day when my new friend would arrive, especially during the times I felt most lonely, and one day it happened. We got to know each other by playing, taking walks together, and spending time with our people. It was hard to get to know him through all his puppy energy.

"Eventually, I realized it was time to share my buried bone with my new friend. I gave it to him, and it still serves as a reminder of how important friendship is to me."

Planning is like burying a bone: envisioning the future, nurturing growth, and enjoying the treasures that come from patience and perseverance.

Endless Opportunities

“When you get in the habit of doing a lot of the same things every day, it can be hard to remember that there’s a whole world outside.

“Chasing the birds, going on a hike, finding a new friend, meeting a new trainer at daycare ... all these things are opportunities to enrich my life and forge new connections.”

Unlock the door to boundless adventure. In every familiar routine lies the potential for exhilarating new experiences and meaningful connections.

Giving Yourself Full Permission to Make Mistakes

"One time, I was playing with my sister, and we broke one of Mom's picture frames. I don't even remember bumping into the table, we were running so fast!

"Mom was really upset, and I felt bad. Eventually, she started petting my head and told me it was okay. She let me go outside and run around for a while to get all my energy out."

I give myself the grace to make mistakes. They're often the fuel for growth and the canvas for learning.

Making Your Voice Heard

"Don't be afraid of using your voice.

"It's okay to advocate for the things you need."

"Dad, can you open the door?" asked Zeus. "I need to go outside."

Recognize the power of your voice, even in the quiet of night. Advocating for your needs is not only okay, it's essential for a fulfilling life.

Successfully Fixing While You're Flying

"The last time we had company over, I got so excited that I couldn't help but jump all over our guests. Mom yelled at me for being too enthusiastic.

"I didn't want to scare our visitors, so I watched how calmly my sister greeted the guests and learned from her.

"Now, when we have company, I take a deep breath, wag my tail, and greet everyone with gentle paws, making sure to show my excitement in a friendly way."

The best adaptations can be made in flight, guided by the wisdom of those around us.

Wanting What Others Have

"Remember when I stole your bone and it turned out to be just like mine?" asked Zeus.

"Yeah, you looked pretty silly," said Aryanna. "But it taught you to appreciate what you have, right?"

"Exactly! Now I savor every chew."

Appreciate the bone you're chewing on. Sometimes what others have isn't any better than what's already in your possession.

Playing with the Birds

"What games do you like?" Zeus asked the birds in the tree. "I'm sure we can find one we both enjoy! Being friends means enjoying our differences too."

Through acceptance and curiosity, even the birds and I find common ground for playful friendship.

Living on the Other Side of Risk

"Hey, what if we go beyond the hill today?" asked Aryanna. "There might be new sticks and new friends!"

"But it's new ... and big," said Zeus. "What if it's too much?"

"That's the fun part! New adventures mean new joys. We won't know until we try, right?"

Life's greatest treasures often await on the other side of fear. Embrace the unknown, for within it lies the magic of new friendships and adventures, worthy of a well-deserved nap.

Life with Mom and Dad

Leadership is best expressed through kindness, respect, and understanding. When there is harmony in a group, it grows from thoughtful guidance rather than control. Those who lead with love and patience inspire others to listen, learn, and support one another, creating an environment where everyone feels valued. In this way, relationships flourish, and the strength of the pack becomes greater than the sum of its parts.

Shared adventures and experiences deepen bonds in unforgettable ways. Whether journeying far or staying close to home, the heart of each adventure lies in the joy of togetherness. By making space for one another, both physically and emotionally, families and friends create lasting memories that go beyond the destination. It's in the moments of laughter, companionship, and mutual support that true fulfillment is found.

At the heart of it all is a sense of belonging and the warmth that comes from being part of something bigger. Whether welcoming guests or simply enjoying the quiet at the end of a long day, there is comfort in knowing that every connection adds to the fabric of home. It is through these moments of connection—both grand and simple—that life's deepest joys are uncovered.

Leading with Love

“At our house, Mom and Dad are the alphas,” said Zeus. “When Jazz and Aryanna first joined the family, they wanted to be alphas.

“Beau and I were better listeners right from the start.

“Our philosophy is when someone does something wrong, you correct them, but you don’t necessarily have to tell them no.

“This makes it easier for us to communicate, respect each other’s boundaries, and live together in harmony.”

Kinship thrives when leaders and followers interact with respect, allowing us to learn and grow under their watchful eyes.

Packing Light, Traveling Together

"Mom and Dad will occasionally leave us behind when they go on trips, and I miss them so much while they are away!" said Zeus.

"Some of my favorite memories, though, are when we get to travel together. My first clue that we're about to go on an adventure is my parents pull out their suitcases. When that happens, I can barely keep my tail still.

"Mom and Dad have to pack extra light so that we can fit in the car together, but they tell us that's what families do for one another. They don't mind making room for us.

"There's a dog-friendly hotel that we love to visit with a big porch. The people who work there know us and remember us every time we come. They make us feel like we are a part of their pack whenever we are there.

"We go to a lot of different places together: the Adirondacks to see the leaves in the fall (even though they all look gray to me, Mom and Dad swear they are beautiful); Ithaca gorges to listen to music; the Berkshires to enjoy some fresh air and beautiful scenery. It doesn't matter where we go, though. The best part is that we can all experience life together."

Every journey is sweeter with family by our side.

Finding Comfort in Quiet Moments

"At the end of every day, we turn on the TV and snuggle in bed or on the couch," said Aryanna.

"It seems so simple: Mom and Dad in their bed, Zeus curled up next to them, and me in my own bed. But, in many ways, this is the most magical part of the day.

"This cozy routine lets us cherish the warmth and companionship of our family, whether we're sharing laughter, quiet moments, or just drifting off to sleep."

In the quiet beauty of ordinary moments, we gather at day's end, finding wonder in simply being together.

Life is wonderful ...
there's just so much to drool about!

Acknowledgments

Where to begin? This book is woven from countless threads of experiences, insights, and moments from my life's journey, all of which have come together on these pages.

It all began with my parents, who allowed us the joy of caring for animals of all kinds—dogs, cats, birds, even a monkey and a horse. Through these relationships, I learned to connect without words, developing a deep intuition that became a kind of "sixth sense."

I am endlessly grateful to the teachers—both literal and figurative—who guided me along the way. At West Junior High in Brentwood, NY, I was fortunate to have inspiring mentors: Mr. Cooper, who made English an adventure; Mr. Hardman, who taught me the life lesson of "Grasping the Nettle," which I carry with me to this day; and Mrs. Harris, whose elegance and wisdom left me with the reminder that "Behind every good man is an AMAZING woman"—a lesson she delivered in heels! These teachers, along with so many others, enriched my life and taught me values I cherish.

It was also in that school that I met Joan Haglund, who introduced me to Buckley and, unknowingly, sparked my lifelong journey with Great Danes.

In my work as a leadership coach, I often talk about "Leader of Self" and encourage people to reflect on the values they live by and the people who exemplify them. Here are five qualities that shaped me, along with the incredible people who demonstrated them:

- **LOVE:** My grandmother, who emigrated from Poland.
- **HARD WORK:** My father, who fled communism in search of freedom.
- **RELATIONSHIPS:** Fran Swete, my boss at Crouse Irving Memorial Hospital.
- **TEAMWORK:** Larry Higbee, who hired me out of my MBA program.
- **COMMUNITY:** Chuckie Holstein, a true leader whose impact has touched countless lives.

I've also been blessed with extraordinary life partners. My husband, Bob Stone, was my rock, supporting me in my ambitions, including my MBA. His only request? That I quit my job to pursue it—so I did.

After Bob's passing, the universe brought Frank Wretzel into my life. His steadfast encouragement has been a pillar of strength for me, enabling the pursuit of new paths—my business, a TEDx talk, and, ultimately, this book. Frank has been endlessly supportive, even through the weekends and weeks I spent away on personal development. From resilience training at Kripalu with Maria Sirois to Positive Psychology training through the WholeBeing Institute with Tal Ben-Shahar, coaching certifications, and numerous workshops, Frank has been by my side, holding me—both literally and figuratively—through it all.

Frank has also shared in my love of Great Danes. He opened his heart first to Jazz, our rescue, and soon after, he suggested we adopt a puppy, intuitively sensing that Jazz needed a companion. Before long, our family grew to include little Beau.

As I ventured into entrepreneurship, I found incredible allies. To Dr. Rick Tamlyn and the ProduceU team, who encouraged me to "Go before you know"—thank you for your wisdom and support. Jono Chowdhury, thank you for always urging me to bring more of myself into my work with your familiar refrain: "Bob, [Barb in his English accent] they need to hear more of you." You have helped me embrace so many things that were not in my "Zone of Genius."

Special thanks to community organizations like Chambers and the WISE Women's Center for their support, and to my family, friends, former colleagues, and mentors who believed in me and helped me grow.

To God and the Universe, who always seemed to open the right doors at the right time.

And to the AMAZING team who made this book possible: Avril King, our editor—thank you for bringing clarity to my ideas. Kristina VanOss, our illustrator—thank you for capturing the spirit of our Great Danes on each page, becoming an extension of my own vision.

With deep gratitude to each of you, whose guidance, love, and inspiration have shaped not only this book but also the person I've become.

Question? Ideas? Stories of your own? Share them with me! Scan the QR code below and send me an email. I would love to hear from you.

Scan the QR code

Meet Jazz, Beau, Aryanna, and Zeus—four lovable canines whose experiences offer a wealth of dog wisdom. In this inspirational collection, Jazz breaks free from her past, Beau faces challenges with loyalty and strength, Aryanna's playful spirit leads her on a path of independence, and Zeus, the bright younger brother, learns the power of adaptability. Their personal growth stories guide readers in overcoming challenges with mindfulness and courage. The pack's insights create a touching compilation for both adults and kids, filled with joyful moments, lessons in resilience, and timeless wisdom—an ideal companion for anyone facing life's transitions and seeking personal growth.

www.ingramcontent.com/pod-product-compliance
Lightning Source LLC
Chambersburg PA
CBHW080052060425
24638CB00003B/3
* 9 7 8 1 9 6 1 7 5 7 9 2 9 *